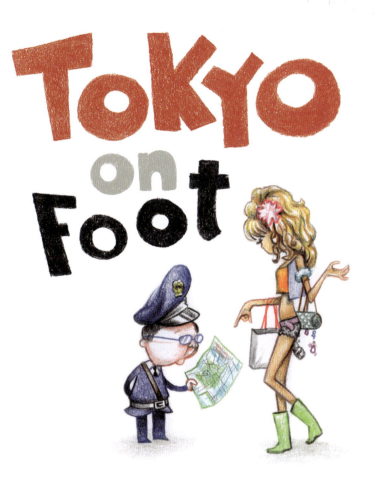

TOKYO on Foot

東京散歩

Travels in the city's most colorful neighborhoods

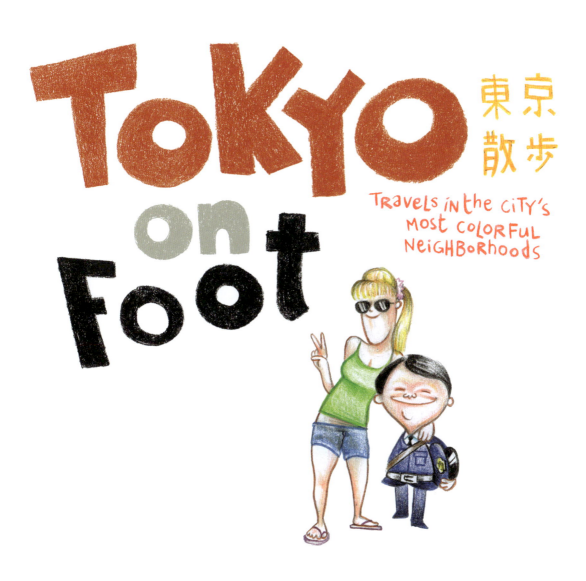

TEXT AND ILLUSTRATIONS BY

FLORENT CHAVOUET

TUTTLE Publishing

Tokyo | Rutland, Vermont | Singapore

Published by Tuttle Publishing, an imprint of Periplus Editions (HK) Ltd.

www.tuttlepublishing.com

Copyright © 2009 by Editions Philippe Picquier
English-language translation copyright © 2011 by Periplus Editions (HK) Ltd.

All rights reserved. No part of this publication may be reproduced or utilized in any form or by any means, electronic or mechanical, including photocopying, recording, or by any information storage and retrieval system, without prior written permission from the publisher.

Library of Congress Cataloging-in-Publication Data
Chavouet, Florent.
 [Tokyo sanpo. English]
 Tokyo on foot : travels in the city's most colorful neighborhoods/text and illustrations by Florent Chavouet.—1st English language ed.
    206 p. : col. ill. ; 26 cm.
  ISBN 978-4-8053-1137-0 (pbk.)
 1. Tokyo (Japan)—Description and travel. 2. Chavouet, Florent—Travel—Japan—Tokyo. 3. Tokyo (Japan)—Social life and customs. 4. City and town life—Japan—Tokyo. 5. Neighborhoods—Japan—Tokyo. 6. Walking—Japan—Tokyo. 7. Cycling—Japan—Tokyo. 8. Tokyo (Japan)—Pictorial works. 9. Tokyo (Japan)—Guidebooks. I. Title.
 DS896.35.C4413 2011
 915.2'135045—dc22
                        2010033405

ISBN 978-4-8053-1137-0
ISBN 978-4-8053-1903-1 (for sale in Japan)

Distributed by

North America, Latin America & Europe
Tuttle Publishing
364 Innovation Drive
North Clarendon, VT 05759-9436 U.S.A.
Tel: 1 (802) 773-8930; Fax: 1 (802) 773-6993
info@tuttlepublishing.com
www.tuttlepublishing.com

Japan
Tuttle Publishing
Yaekari Building, 3rd Floor
5-4-12 Osaki, Shinagawa-ku, Tokyo 141 0032
Tel: (81) 3 5437-0171; Fax: (81) 3 5437-0755
sales@tuttle.co.jp
www.tuttle.co.jp

Asia Pacific
Berkeley Books Pte. Ltd.
3 Kallang Sector #04-01, Singapore 349278
Tel: (65) 6741-2178; Fax: (65) 6741-2179
inquiries@periplus.com.sg
www.tuttlepublishing.com

First English-language edition
28 27 26 25 24   15 14 13 12 11   2408EP

Printed in China

TUTTLE PUBLISHING® is a registered trademark of Tuttle Publishing, a division of Periplus Editions (HK) Ltd.

Tokyo is said to be the most beautiful of ugly cities. Those seeking old stone buildings won't find their quota of medieval streets and historical districts there, but they will still leave with the satisfied feeling of having filled their eyes (while having emptied their wallets).

There are, of course, many things to see in Tokyo. For me to say which to visit would be to predigest part of the trip for you; and besides, curiosity is much too individual a trait to take directions.

Which suits me just fine. I wouldn't know how to squeeze a glimpse of the city's many characteristics into the space of a preface. At best I would offer this thought, that it's better to be amused by the little things than to walk away from them. In Tokyo, and in Japan in general, the disoriented feeling of being in a foreign land comes from the slightly silly state of awareness that makes us admire a road sign just because it's different from the ones we're familiar with, or a fruit label because we can't understand what's written on it.

So this is a book about Japan. About a trip to Tokyo, to be precise. It's neither a guide nor an adventure story, but that doesn't mean you'll avoid the out-of-date addresses of the one or the digressive confidences of the other. I stayed in Tokyo from June to December 2006, which corresponded exactly to the duration of my partner Claire's internship there, the primary reason for this trip.

   Since I really didn't have much to do and was reluctant to earn my keep taking on any number of meaningless jobs, I started to draw, with no particular goal in mind. Accompanied by my two most faithful friends, a lady's bicycle and a folding chair, I went scouring the streets to see what my new surroundings looked like.

   One thing for sure, it's a known fact that a bike is the best means for exploring a city, and it doesn't lead to sore feet. You can befriend taxi drivers with hand gestures, and you benefit from better views than from the window of a Yamanote train. So the only advice I would give to future eager visitors is to pack your bike in your bag—though on foot you see a lot too.

   However, no matter how hard I pedaled or how willing my pencils were, I wasn't able to cover all the streets of Tokyo, one more way in which I resembled the local taxi drivers. The Tokyo depicted here is strongly colored by my day-to-day experiences as well as my moods, and I apologize in advance if it doesn't correspond in every respect to the real thing. My take is but one of many visions of the city that travelers can turn to.

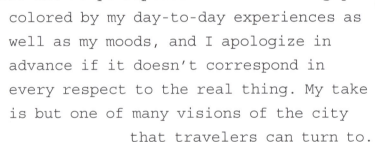
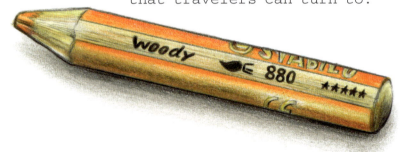

The book in your hands is organized as follows. Each chapter corresponds to a neighborhood I visited. The respective lengths of the chapters in no way indicate the relative importance of the neighborhoods in the life of the city but rather my familiarity with them.

Hand-drawn maps that are admittedly quite personal in their details introduce the neighborhoods, and on them I've marked the chapter's illustrations. I leave it to the sticklers out there to confirm whether my drawings do justice to their subjects. Finally, each chapter is announced by a koban, the local police branch station. Again, a very personal choice.

The koban is to Japanese architecture what the monuments of World War One were to French artists: a large source of commissions in which the deciding criteria were considerably more lenient than usual. For this reason, kobans offer a range of more or less recent, more or less studied styles and genres, which dot the landscape of Tokyo. The interior of the koban is, however, unvarying: the chipped furniture, the neighborhood map, the portrait gallery of most-wanted criminals, and the fine team of policemen handing out directions to passersby.

Given their usual pastime, these good officers won't mind if I use them here to introduce chapters.

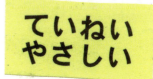

As for the rest, I leave it to you to discover for yourself.

During the six months that I spent in Tokyo trying to absorb and understand a bit of the world around me, I remained a tourist nonetheless. With the constant feeling of not quite "getting" everything I didn't know, and the odd habit of pasting fruit labels everywhere, because I had no idea what was written on them.

On my return to France, people asked me if China was nice. To which I responded that, in any case, the Japanese there were very friendly.

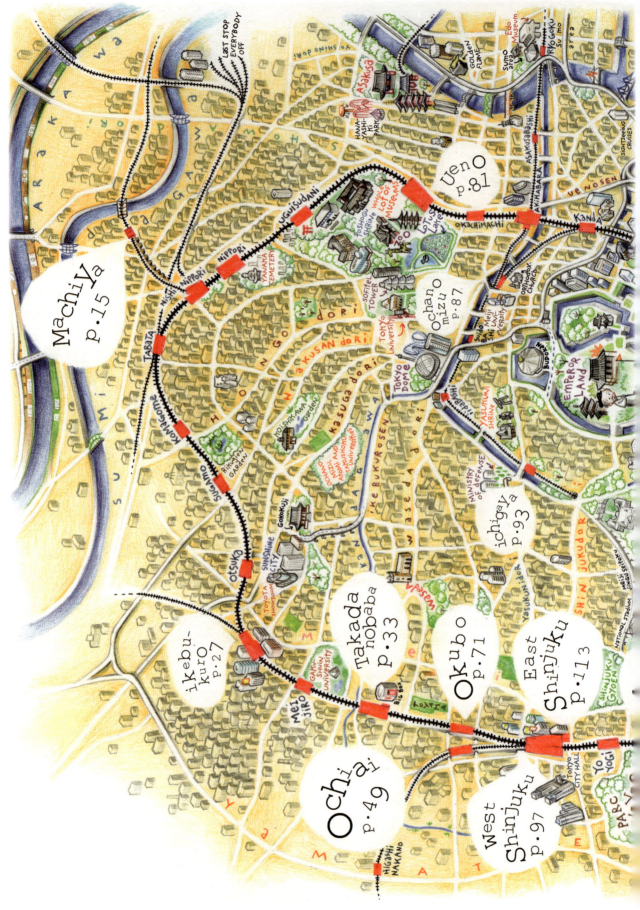

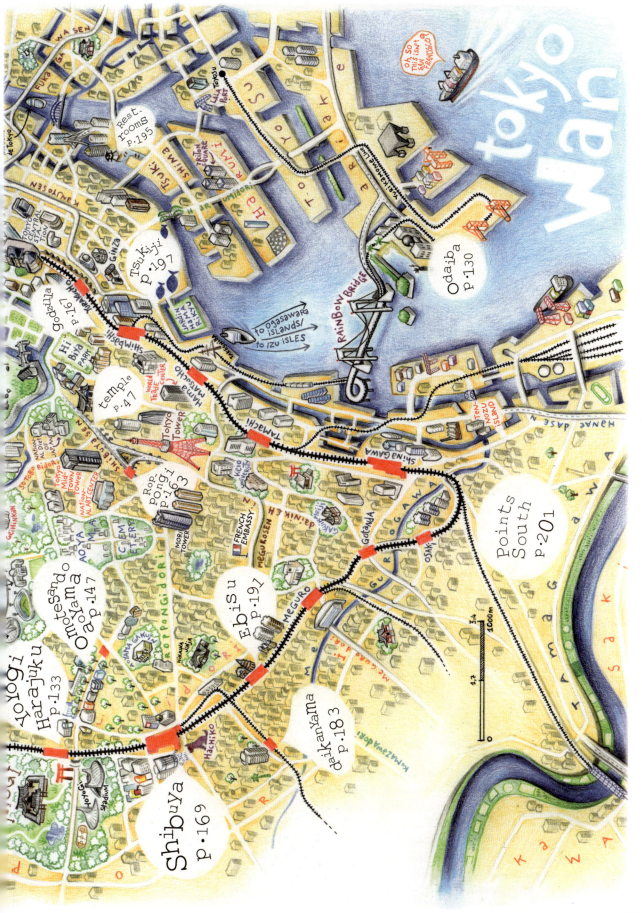

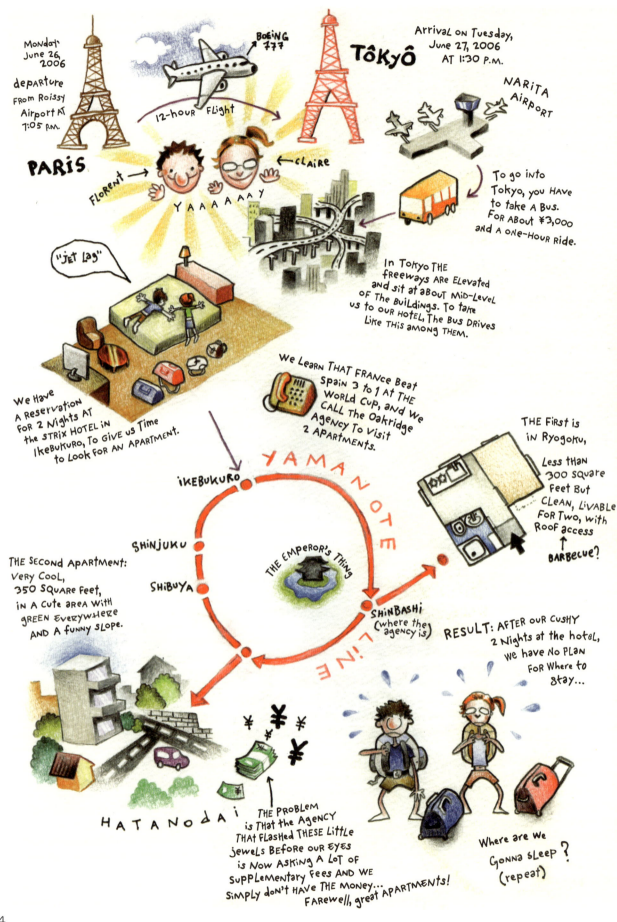

IN MACHIYA!

Claire got back in touch with an agency that deals in "guest houses," i.e. shared houses. We took the first one, which was also one of the cheapest, in Machiya, an area full of moms, way to the north and pretty far from downtown. We rented 2 tatami rooms. We have a place, and a roof over our heads.

Cheap joke:

Every morning we're woken up by the sound of a mini-keyboard. I'm trying to imagine the face of the guy (or ♀) who always plays the same melody, at 8 in the morning. With false notes too!

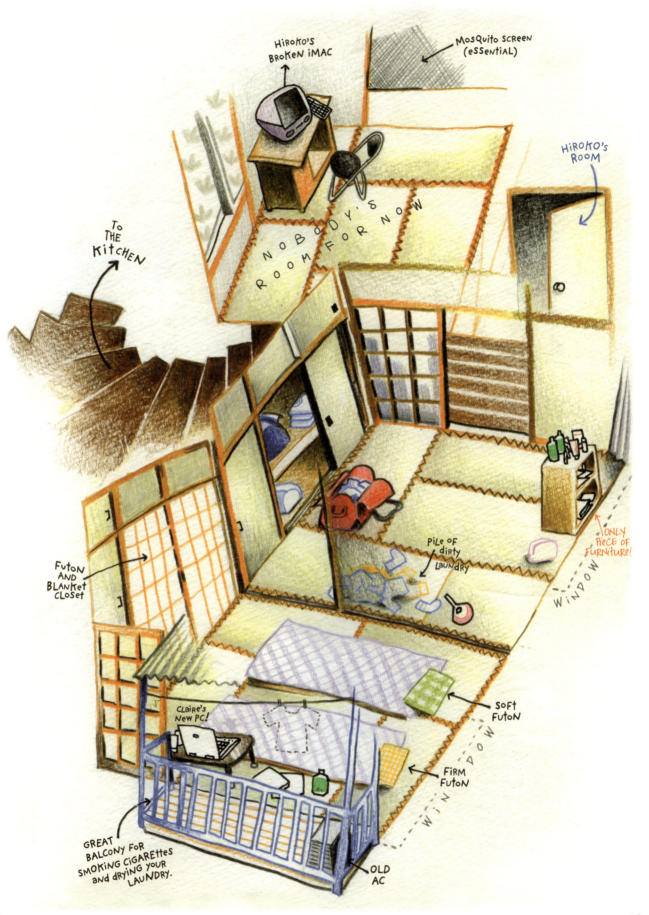

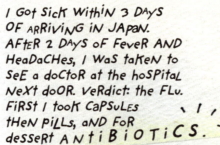

I got sick within 3 days of arriving in Japan. After 2 days of fever and headaches, I was taken to see a doctor at the hospital next door. Verdict: the flu. First I took capsules then pills, and for dessert ANTIBIOTICS.

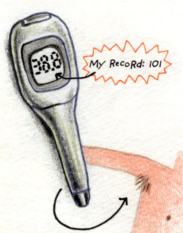

My record: 101

In Japan the armpits are the baby's behind.

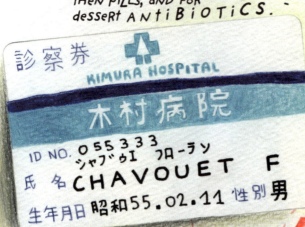

YUMMY

Which means I drew all the preceding pages and some of the following ones with my health doing a yoyo.

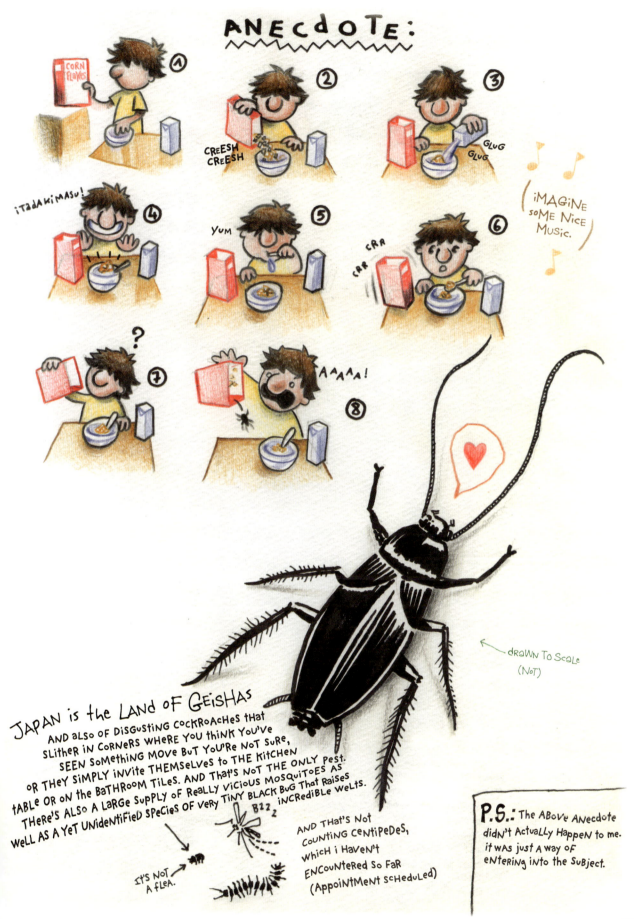

TODAY Little Kim sent 7 firecrackers into the sea of Japan.

Seen on the banks of the Arakawa: a lady walking her pet pig.

"Are you coming, Maxie?"

白洋舍
CLEAN LIVING

"i am socié."

movie star sophie marceau is stealing work from movie star jean reno doing ads.

is she socié too?

"Hey, this one's specially for you."

i found this golf ball in a patch of clover. japanese play golf a lot along with another boring sport, baseball. but everybody knows that.

↑ a more likely explanation.

an altus NEWING number 8!!!

YAAAAAAAAaaY!

Hmm... is it worth anything?

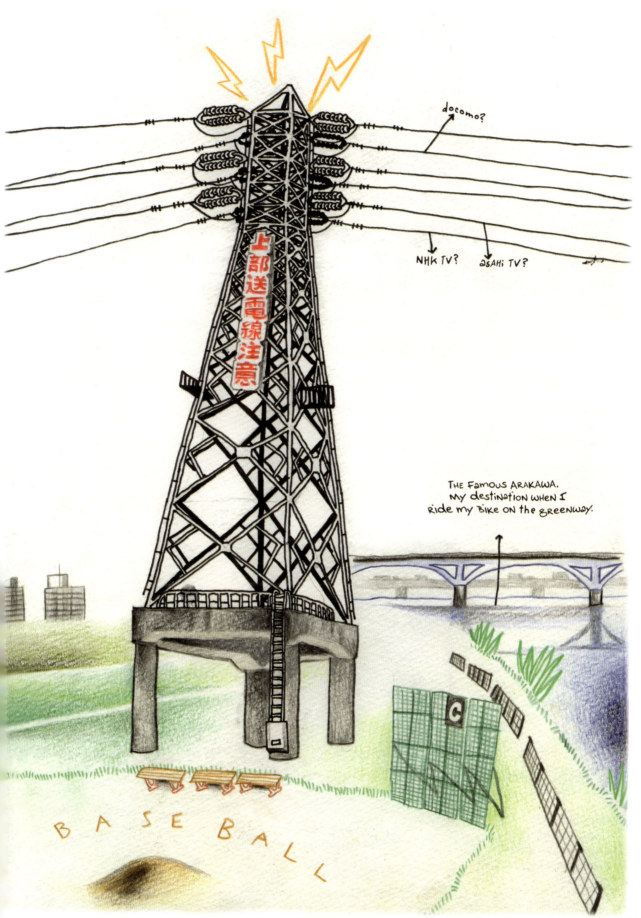

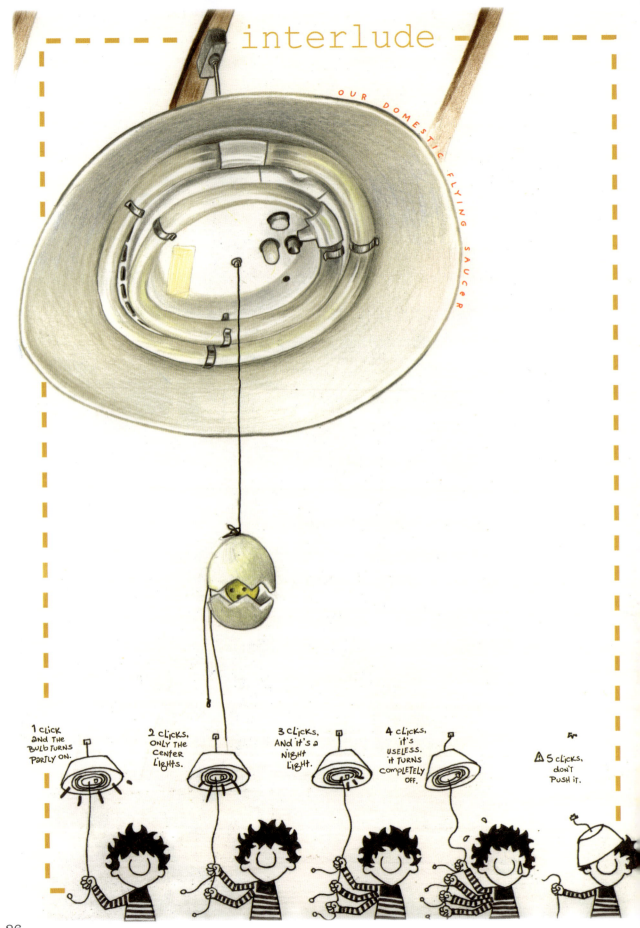

interlude

Today I'm playing tourist in a manga bookstore. To judge only by the covers (since you can't open the books), the main themes are:
- Porn (soft, hard, kinky, gay...)
- Romantic stuff
- And some sports.

Slight disappointment: in the (short) aisle of foreign comics, there are only American comics and art books.

"I can't believe it!"
"That's impossible!"

MACHIYA
In all, we stayed there only 2 weeks.
Machiya was way over there

IKEBUKURO
TAKADANOBABA
YAMANOTE
SHINJUKU
SHIBUYA

EMPEROR →

Oh, by the way!
We've moved. We now live in a new guest house, but this time in Takadanobaba, near Shinjuku, much closer to the center of Tokyo. But I'll draw the house some other time.

In any case, no more keyboard at 7 a.m.!

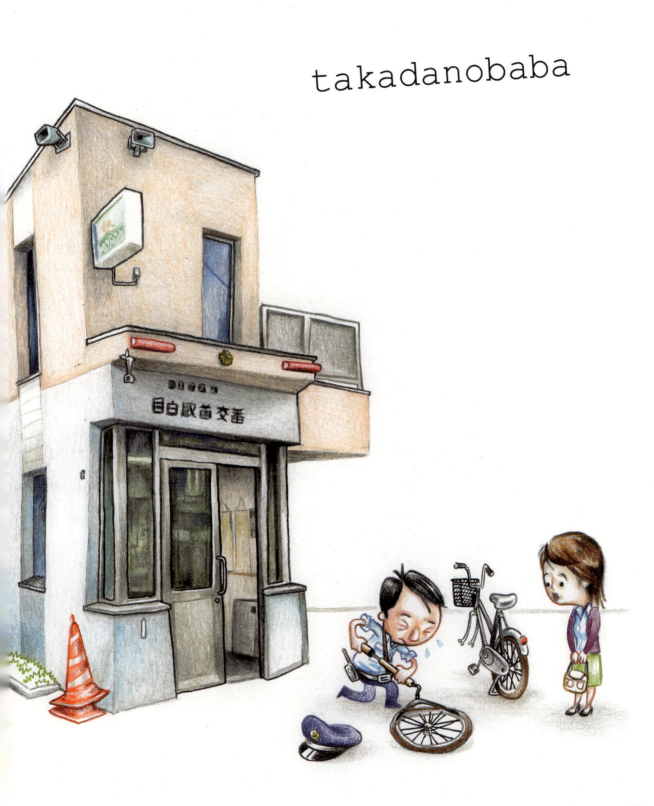

takadanobaba

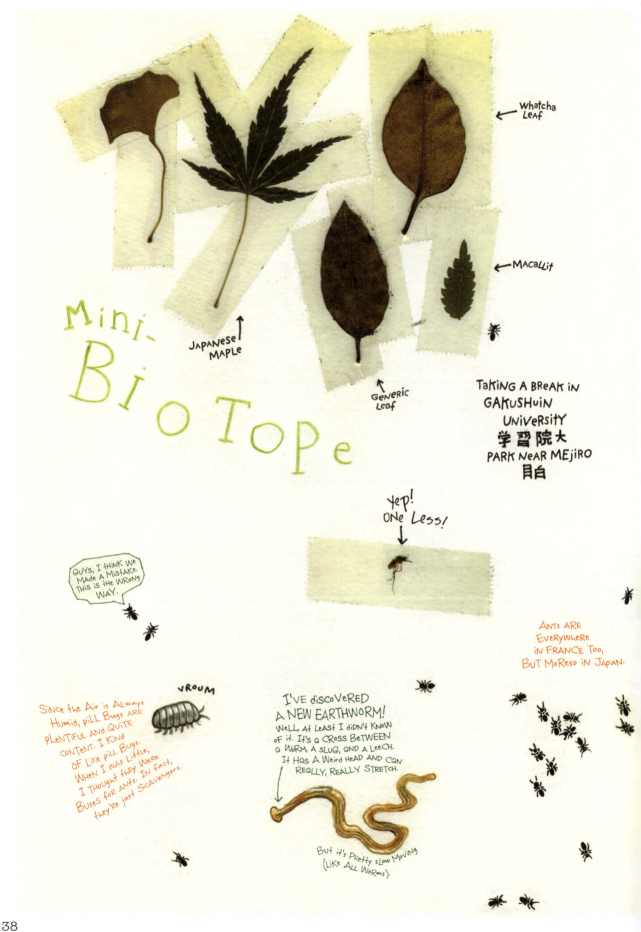

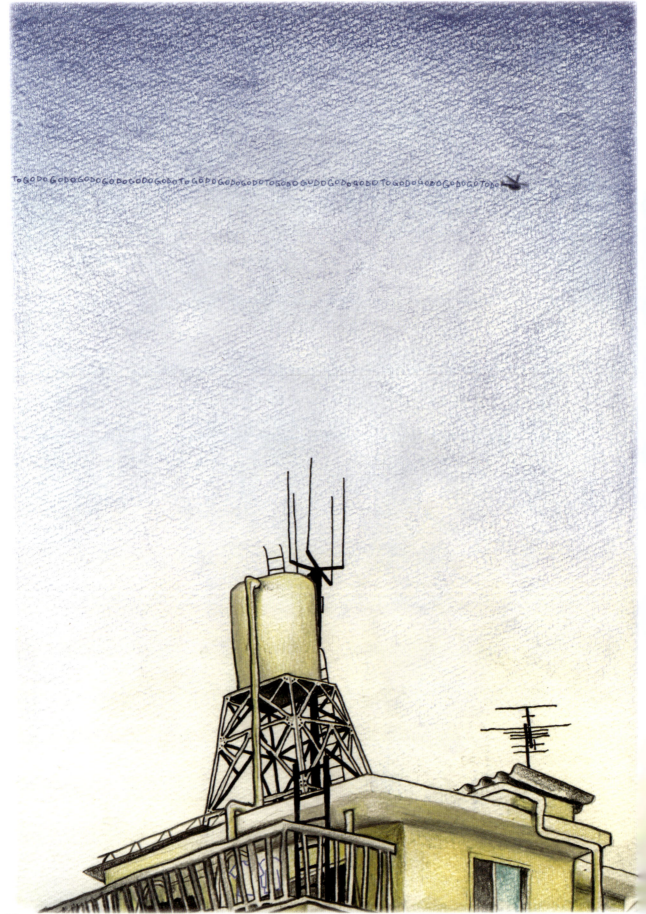

interlude

SOMEONE TOLD ME THAT, A FEW YEARS AGO, RINGO STARR APPEARED IN AN AD FOR APPLES IN JAPAN. THANKS TO THAT, I CAN ALWAYS REMEMBER THAT RINGO MEANS "APPLE" IN JAPANESE.

THE JAPANESE APPLE

HERE, LOTS OF THINGS ARE EXPENSIVE, ESPECIALLY FRUITS:
To be MORE SPECIFIC AND to prove that I'm RIGHT, I went to the LOCAL SUPERMARKET ARMED WITH A LITTLE NOTEBOOK, IN ORDER TO WRITE DOWN THE PRICES IN THE FRUIT SECTION:
CANTALOUPES, BETWEEN ¥598 AND ¥780 DEPENDING ON SIZE (AROUND $6 to $8)
PEARS: ¥398 EACH
A SLICE OF WATERMELON (about a fifth): ¥398
GRAPEFRUIT: VERY CHEAP ¥100, PINK ONES: ¥78
4 WITHERED FIGS: ¥498
3 TOMATOES: ¥298
4 BANANAS ¥298 (that's OKAY)
4 KIWIS: ¥350 OR ¥128 PER KIWI
ONE PEACH (MOMO) ¥398 (4 BUCKS!) But it's TRUE THEY'RE VERY LARGE
A NICE PINEAPPLE: ¥1398!
GRAPES → 3 LITTLE BUNCHES: ¥298
→ Japanese Grapes (BUDO): ¥1,850!!! A BUNCH AS BIG AS YOUR HAND... Roughly 18 BUCKS)
THE AWARD GOES TO THE MANGO: OVER ¥2000 AND IT WAS THE SAME AT ANOTHER, SLIGHTLY LESS TRAFFICKED SUPERMARKET, FOR WHERE IT'S STILL 20 BUCKS FOR A LOUSY PIECE FRUIT.

¥150 (AND that's a BARGAIN). NORMALLY, IT'S AROUND 3 FOR ¥500-600.

AND TO THINK THAT WHEN I WAS LITTLE AND HAD A JOB PICKING APPLES IN THE ORCHARD NEAR WHERE I LIVED, WE'D BITE INTO AN APPLE ONCE, THEN THROW IT AWAY AND GET ANOTHER... ON THE OTHER HAND, RICE IS CHEAP.

FRUIT SALAD, LOVELY, LOVELY LOVELY

around our house (ochiai)

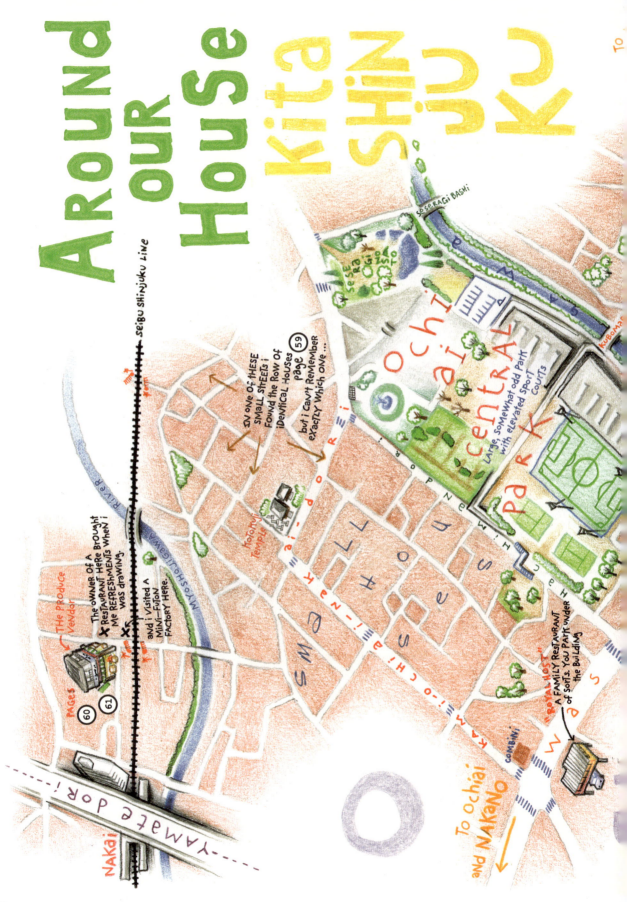

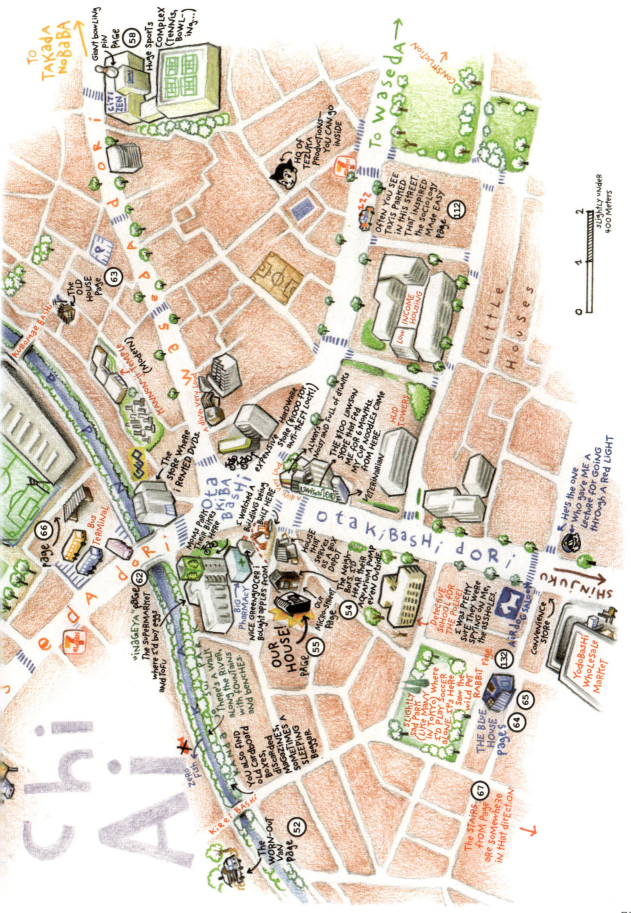

↑ Like the Movie

Little TV Game

Unmold a flan on a guy's eye, and the guy has to swallow it without the aid of his hands, using only eyebrow and jaw movements.

It's doable.

GULP

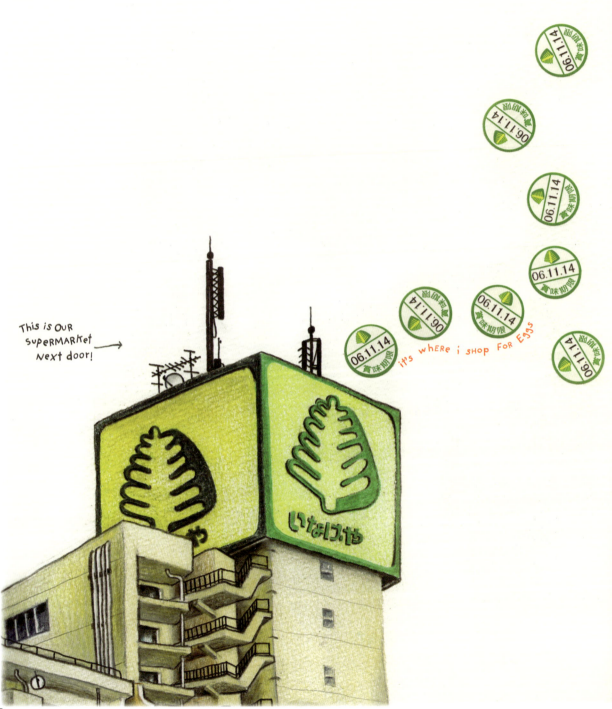

okubo

cwhat?

SEEN ON tHe ROAD between SHiNJuKu aNd YOyogi: 2 CROWS EATiNG A DeAD PiGEON.

SUBARASHii Ai

Claire / Me (Roommate 1) / Menaka / Michiko (Roommate 2)

Claire AND i WeRe just LeAVING OUR pLACE WhEN We WeRe ASSAULteD by A bUNCH OF ladies Who said tHey WeRE KoReANS AND WERE GeNeROUSly iNVITING us to Participate in an "oPeN HOUSe" at tHe BELievers PARiSH NeXt-DooR AND EVEN iF we WeREN't BELievers We'd ReCeive FRee KoReAN beNtO BOX LUNCHES. It WAS tHiS LAST bit tHAT PROMPteD us TO CHECK out WhAT PROVed to be A trAP FoR JeSUS FREAKS, COMPLete With A CONCert of WhAt tHey SHAMeLESSLY CaLLeD GoSPeL MUSic to toP it aLL off.

IMPROVISED KoReAN DAY

We Returned HoMe Without tHe beNto but WiTH A brand New Testament.

YUMMY

ToDAY LiTTLe KiM exPLoded HiS bomb.

SOME CAR NAMES WORTH NOTING:

THE MAJESTA
THE ARISTO
THE SUPER DELUXE CEDRIC (Nissan)
THE SUPER CUSTOM CEDRIC (Nissan)
THE EVERY (Suzuki)
THE MIRA (Fake Micra)
THE DUTRO (Light Truck)
THE ELGRAND (Nissan)
THE EDIX
THE CERVO
THE LAFESTA
THE PRESAGE

i bought it at **TOKYU HANDS** — A big and very popular department store where you can find everything (sort of like target, only better)

interlude

It's self-colored (it's its true color on the sketch)

MemoGraph COLOR PENCIL Tombow 朱-1500

MY NEW BRAND of PENCIL: TOMBOW. It's SUPPOSED TO BE WELL KNOWN. A VERY OLD COMPANY THAT MAKES MARKERS TOO. IN ANY CASE, AND AS OPPOSED TO THE MITSUBISHI ONES I BOUGHT, I'M REALLY HAPPY WITH IT. THE LEAD IS SOLID, AND the PRICE is THE LOWEST ON the SHELF (¥82, I THINK). I ONLY HAVE 2 FOR THE MOMENT, 2 COLORS I DON'T USE MUCH, WHICH is DUMB, BUT at LEAST I'M CONTRIBUTING to the LOCAL ECONOMY. DOWN WITH GERMAN PENCILS!

BIT of JAPANESE FOREST

TABATA Station

Boo Hoo

79

Vignette From Ueno

interlude

釜を見よ！麺に驚き、だしにうなずけ！

讃岐うどん大使
東京麺通団

This is a really good udon restaurant. First you choose the type of udon you want (cold, hot, thick...), the cook gives you the bowl when you come in, and then it's like a cafeteria with your little tray, where you choose toppings (tempura, etc.) to complement your choice. You pay at the end and then you sit

← (in an all-wood interior with a decor that subtly evokes Shikoku, the birthplace of the udon noodle).

BANANA LABEL.

And this is not so good. It's a parking violation sticker that someone is paid to slap onto bikes parked where they shouldn't be (meaning everywhere). →

- - interlude - - -

Cup noodles are like party favor bags. So many goodies inside.

FREEZE-DRIED VEGGIES

OIL

3 POUCHES! THIS ENTIRE FEAST FOR ONLY ¥105

CABBAGE, GREENS, STUFF

MAYONNAISE (SURPRISINGLY POPULAR IN JAPAN)

JAPANESE "BBQ" SAUCE FOR A YAKI-SOBA ATMOSPHERE IN THE HOME

P.S.: Today I was detained because I crossed (a street, on foot) on a red light (for pedestrians).

interlude

My Contribution

— interlude —

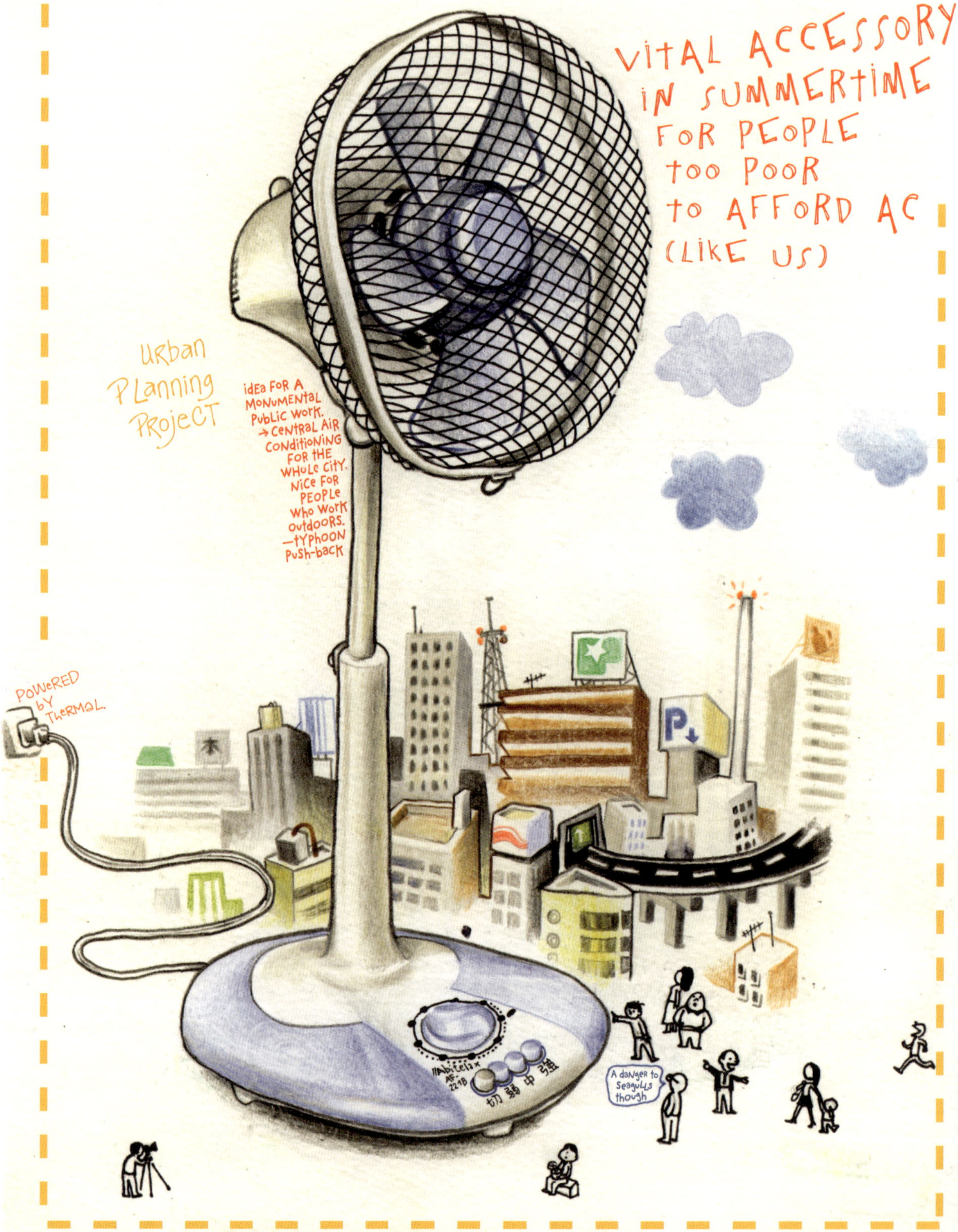

VITAL ACCESSORY IN SUMMERTIME FOR PEOPLE TOO POOR TO AFFORD AC (LIKE US)

URBAN PLANNING PROJECT

idea for a monumental public work. → central air conditioning for the whole city. Nice for people who work outdoors. —typhoon push-back

POWERED by thermal.

A danger to seagulls though

ichigaya

WEST SHINJUKU

TO OCHIAI and TAKADANOBABA ←
"shiddiqi:" Indian Restaurant (You Can Eat Outdoors) →

TO OKUBO ↑ Shokuan dori

Ota — Kiba — Shi dori

A HUMAN TORSO WAS FOUND IN A TRASH CAN IN THIS STREET ONCE. THERE WERE COPS EVERYWHERE, BUT THIS TIME THEY WEREN'T THERE TO TICKET BIKES.

Mr. SADA's BUILDING, ON THE THIRD FLOOR THERE'S A Record Shop

"Little Spoon" Curry Restaurant (108)

THE REALLY GOOD UDON RESTAURANT FROM PAGE 85

FRESHNESSBURGER — A small chain of Hamburger Joints "made on the premises" Rather Good, and the cooks are young and cool (beard)

Always 2 or 3 PEOPLE LOITERING IN FRONT OF this DUMP

WASEDA PREP CLASSES

The Nishi Shinjuku Hotel — Good and Cheap

Shobu Park

CEMETERY

JOEN-JI TEMPLE

CONSTRUCTION

SUPERMARKET

OLD HOUSES

Naruko ten jinja

SCHOOL

I-Land Patio — Quiet place to sip a drink or draw. At night you can watch the cockroaches mate.

I-LAND TOWER

Tokyo Teaching Hospital

Omeki ai d

CONSTRUCTION

I SAW AN ALTAR PUT UP IN LESS THAN 1 WEEK HERE

"HANAMASA" CONSTRUCTION — HANAMASA is a chain of wholesalers for restaurants, but anyone can go and buy MEAT there, and it's CHEAPER than REGULAR SUPERMARKETS.

Mitsui Building

High School

Shinjuku Square Tower

SMALL HOUSES, VACANT LOT, AND

TO NAKANO SAKAUE ↙

AROUND HERE I DREW THE PAY PHONE PAGE (100)

0 1,25 2,5 — about 100 meters

⊙ = KOBAN

98

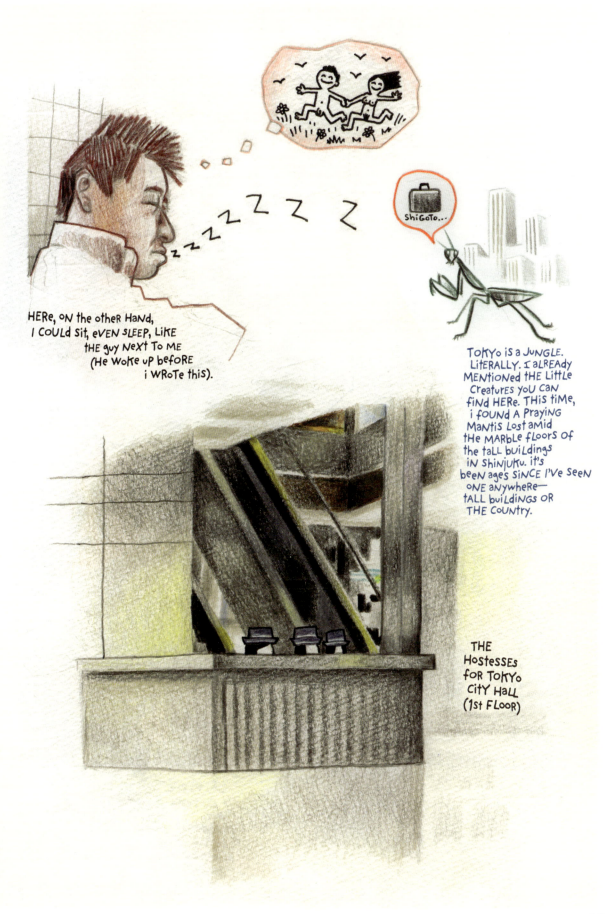

interlude

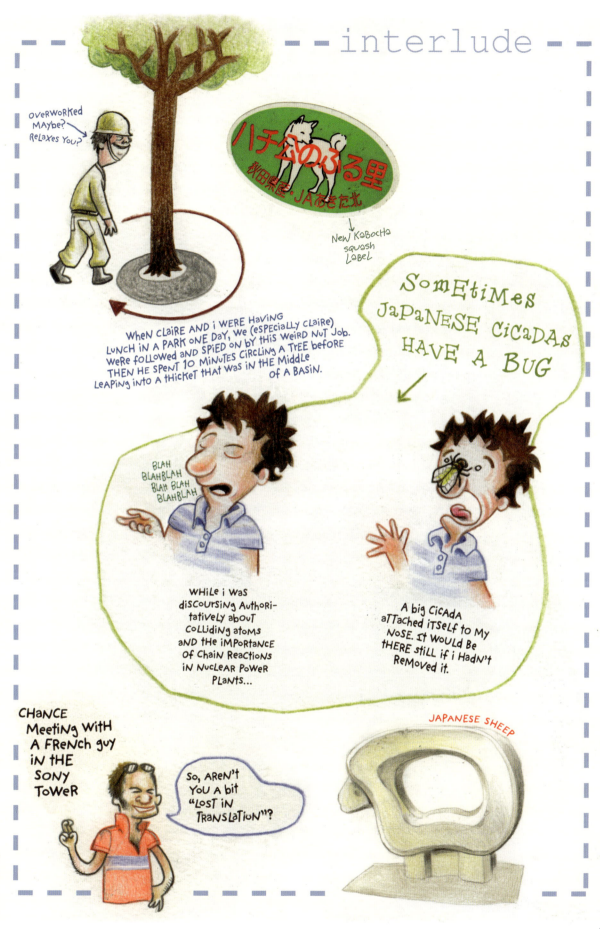

interlude

east shinjuku

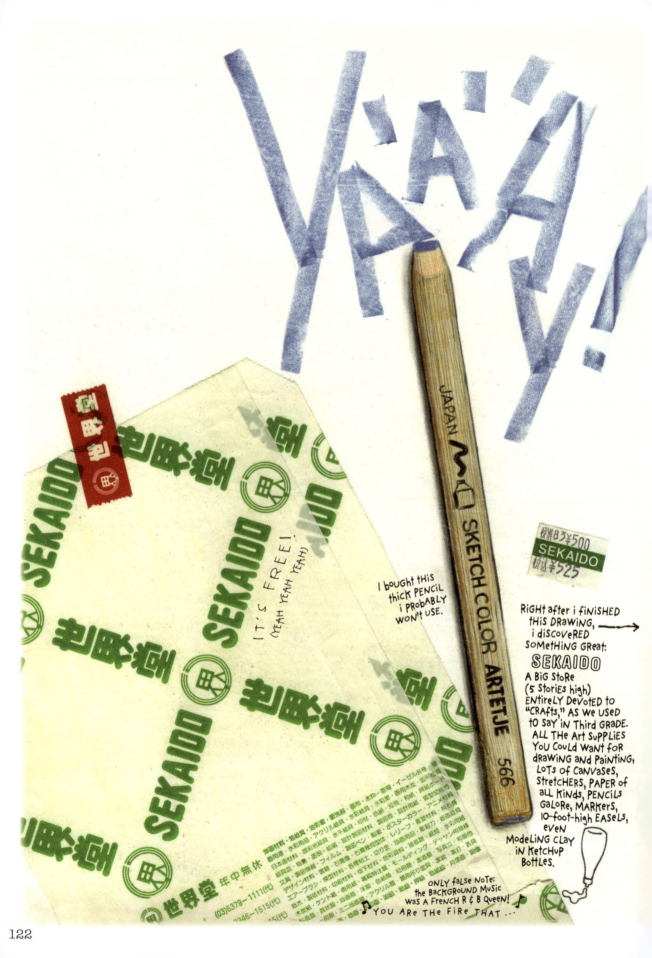

From a Muji store:

the Muji RuBix Cube

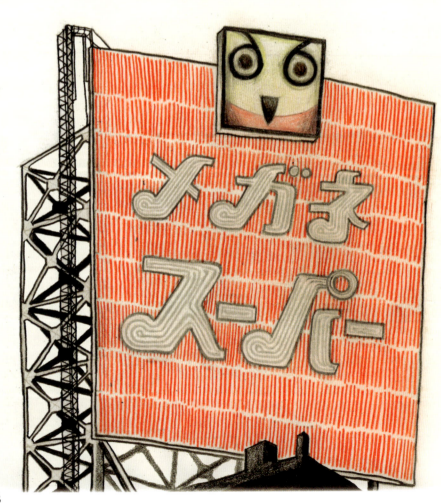

LAZY WEEKEND

☀ 95°F

Since, on top of a whole day spent lounging on the lawn in Shinjuku Gyoen, we went to **ODAIBA** (Tokyo Beach), the megalopolis's gorgeous artificial beach.

To get there, the best (but not only) way is via the RAINBOW BRIDGE, the big suspension bridge that spans the bay. On our way over, we took the monorail. On the way back, we took our feet. Yes, you can walk across it if you stay to the side while sampling the various exquisite muffler pollens.

PACIFIC OCEAN

ODAIBA is a kind of beach resort, with malls, outdoor cafés, a beach, and artificial islands. From a distance, it looks nice, especially when the heat in the city (95 degrees) is unbearable. But when you get closer, it's a letdown. Tokyo being what it is, the water is not blue, it's brown. The sand is not fine, it's mud. You can't see your feet even in water 4 inches deep. Kids aside, no adults in their right mind would think of going in. Well, sailboarders do.

"Where did my feet go?"

Isn't he cute? →

A beautiful male Tahitian lady. →

→ g-string

130

The Sea!

Yes, it's true:
 Tokyo really is a port.
 A big one even.
 But no french-fry vendors
    like back home.

interlude

yoyogi harajuku

interlude

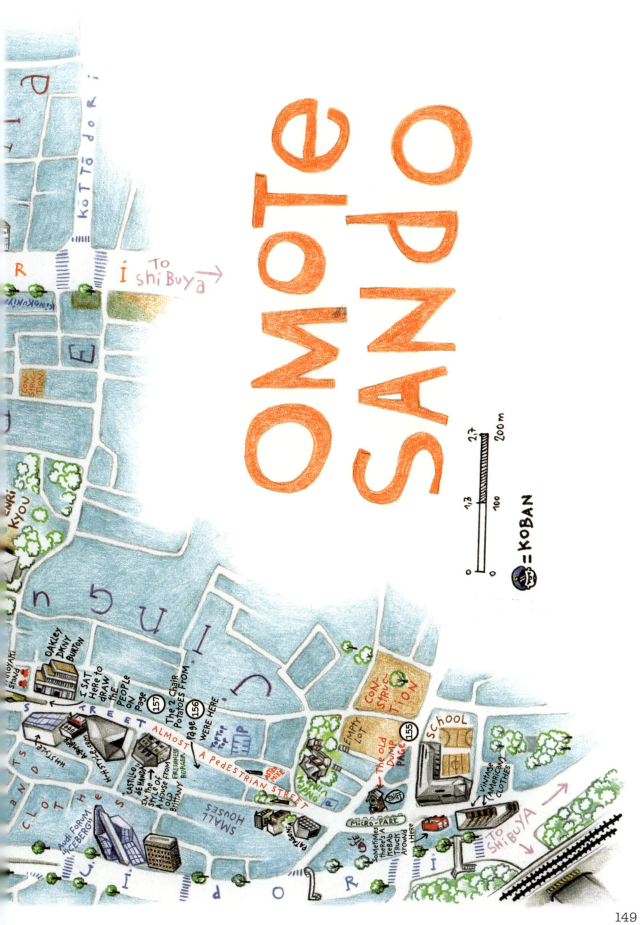

It's raining. So I had to abandon the drawing on the facing page. I'll finish it one day when I can trust the weather. Meanwhile, I've taken shelter in a café-bakery-tea house.

Fake French flag

↓ Doughy inside

← Brioche in the shape of a tartlet with a sugar topping

How does it work?

① I go in and equip myself with tongs and a tray.

② I choose between the rolls, croissants, and pigs in a blanket, which are too tempting.

③ I pay and order a drink if I want one.

④ I park myself and eat.

store window
♥ irony
Near (omotesando)

interlude

Freaky Moment:
(Maybe just a bad joke?)
A "city employee" was ogling us—Claire, one of her friends, and me—with a rather disturbing grin and, what was even more unsettling, holding a chainsaw in his hands.

hee hee.

He reminded us a lot of the weird guy circling the tree.

What?! Another ticket for parking in a no-bike zone!

Very popular guy on TV

Kinky Interlude

Ha Ha, Well Done, Young American Hoodlum

interlude

Cheap joke

fuji films.

Japanese Facial Hair

Sociology Made Easy #4

R & B Hip-Hop Street Wear (Worn only while frowning)

The "Johnny Depp"

The "Perverse Virgin" (A kind of partial Johnny Depp), very common around Akihabara and among convenience store clerks

The "Miyazaki" or "Cool Chimney-Fire Grandpa Retiree" (Rare in Tokyo)

The "Imperial" or body-art contestant

The "Macaque," impressive in the wild, spotted near our local supermarket (Not to be confused with the Woman beggar, though)

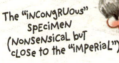

The "Incongruous" Specimen (Nonsensical but close to the "Imperial")

roppongi

interlude

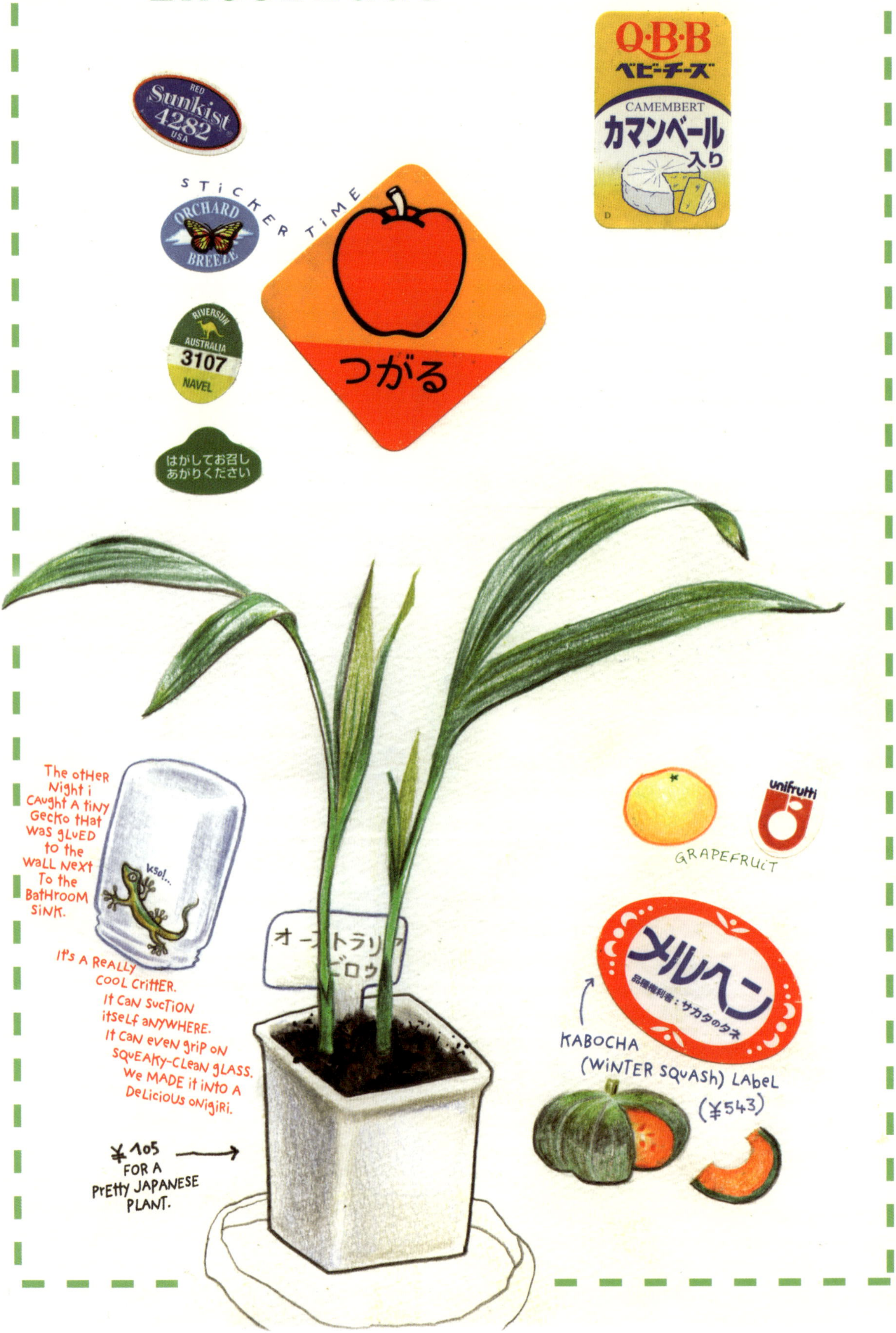

STICKER TIME

はがしてお召し
あがりください

つがる

The other night I caught a tiny gecko that was glued to the wall next to the bathroom sink.

kSSS!...

It's a really cool critter. It can suction itself anywhere. It can even grip on squeaky-clean glass. We made it into a delicious onigiri.

オーストラリア
ビロウ

¥105 → for a pretty Japanese plant.

GRAPEFRUIT

KABOCHA
(WINTER SQUASH) LABEL
(¥543)

shibuya

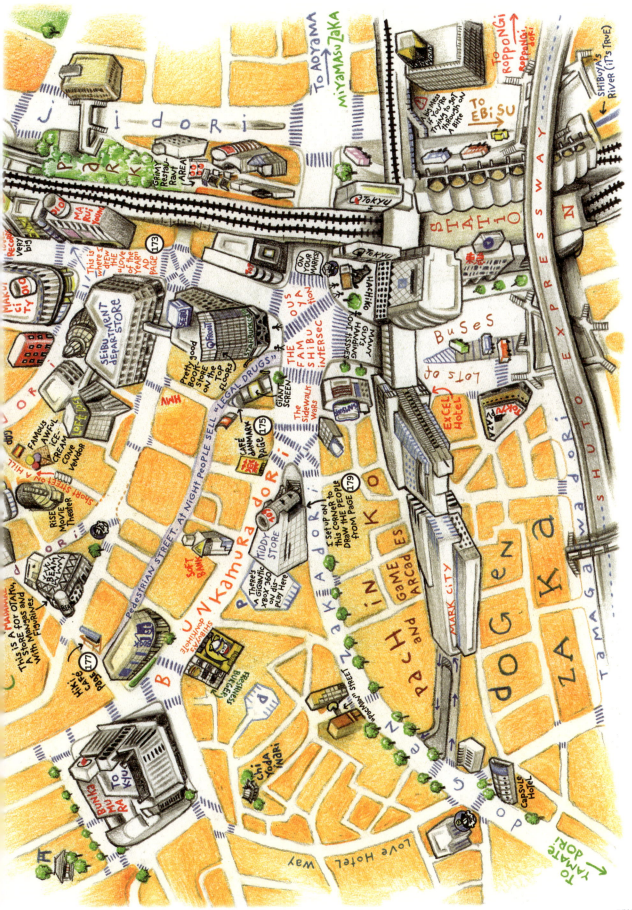

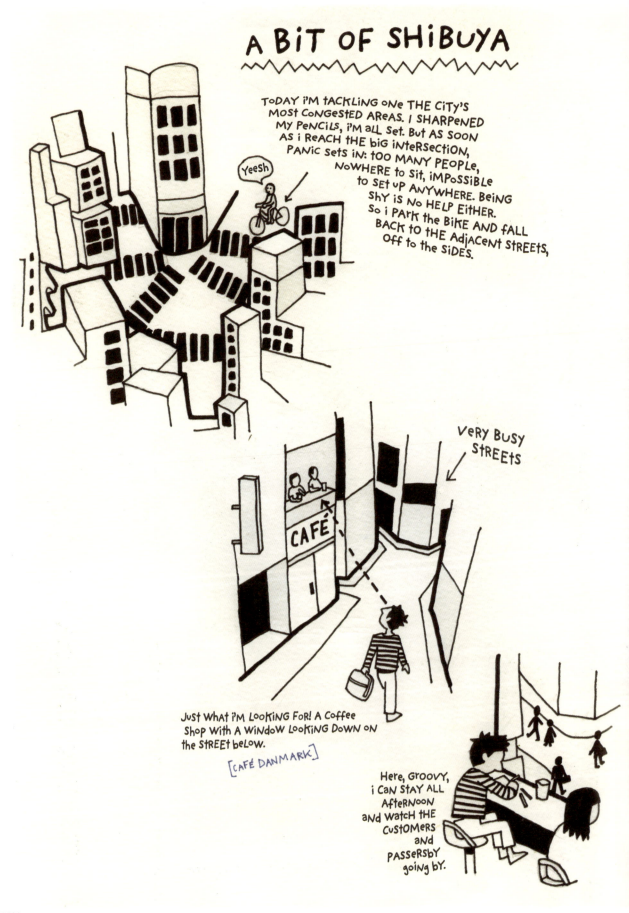

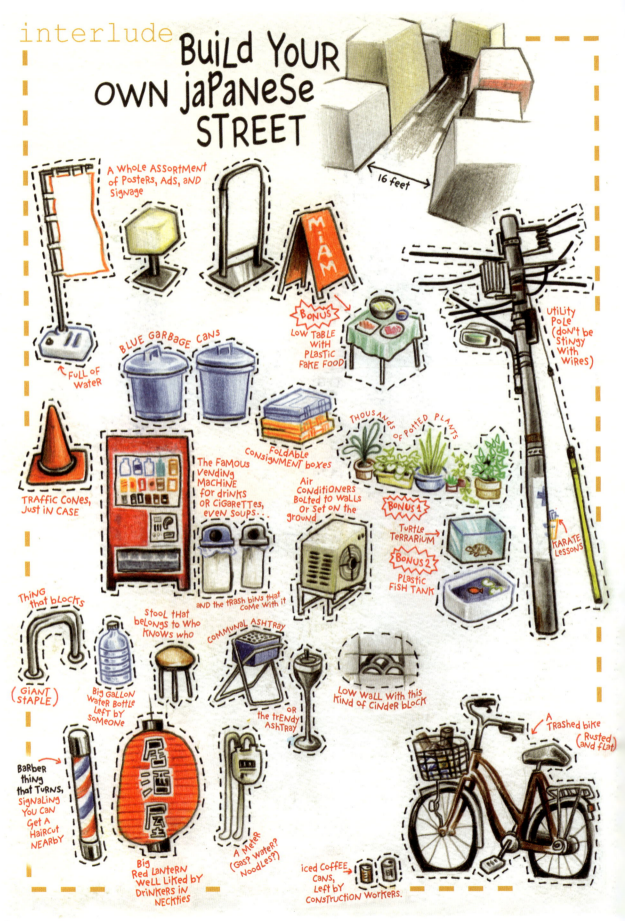

daikanyama

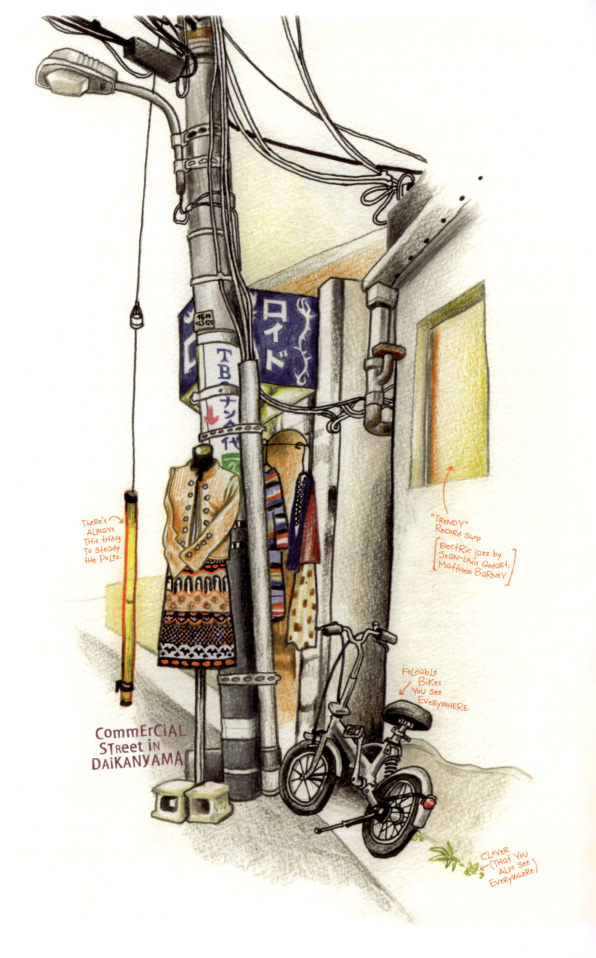

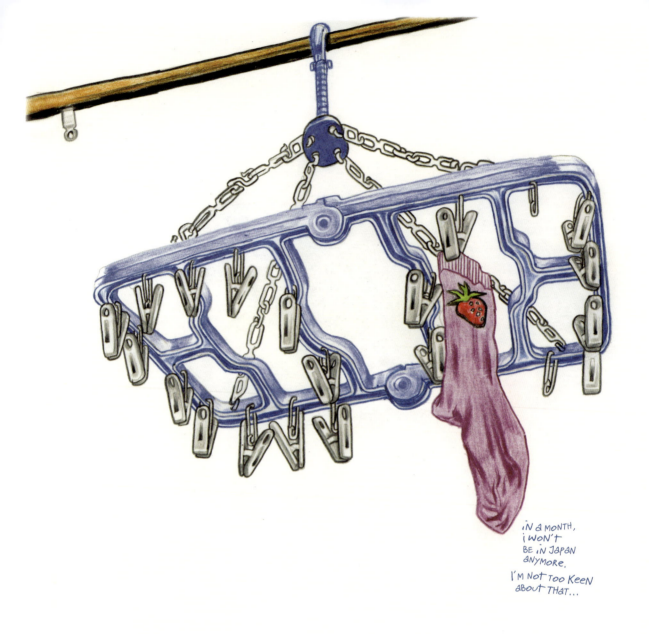

- - - interlude - - - - - - - - - - - - -

interlude

Sociology made easy 5

 Survey of the Koban population: The Kobanese.

THE OLD HAND

THE YOUNG VETERAN

THE FRESH RECRUIT

SYMPATHY	★★	★★★	★
COMMUNICATION	★	★★★	★
DANGEROUSNESS	★★	★	★★★

BEWARE: beneath his wise old grandpa appearance has retained some of the reflexes of his glory days when he pursued and ran down the snatchers of sacks of rice. Has a surplus of moral rectitude ("it is forbidden to cross when the light is red.")

Smiles the most of all and is the most talented at giving directions. Sometimes hesitates to utilize the English he learned during a week-long camping trip in New Zealand once. He's the one who drives the car.

Very proud of her illuminated baton. Fantasizes about Al-Qaeda Korean terrorists and chomps at the bit while waiting for her big break (the theft of the daily earnings from a drinks vending machine)

interlude

ebisu

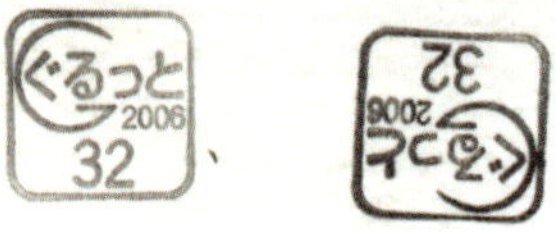

interlude

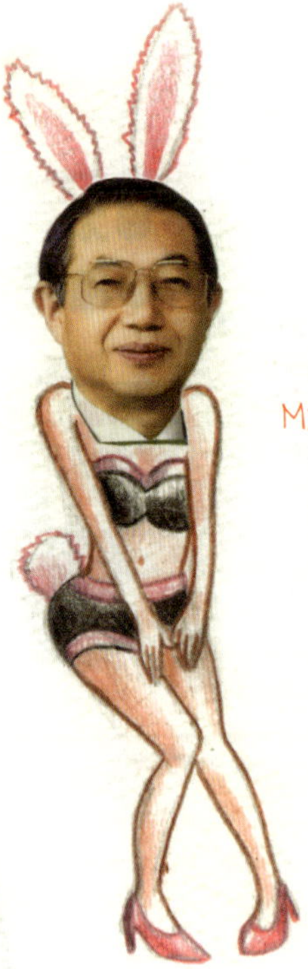

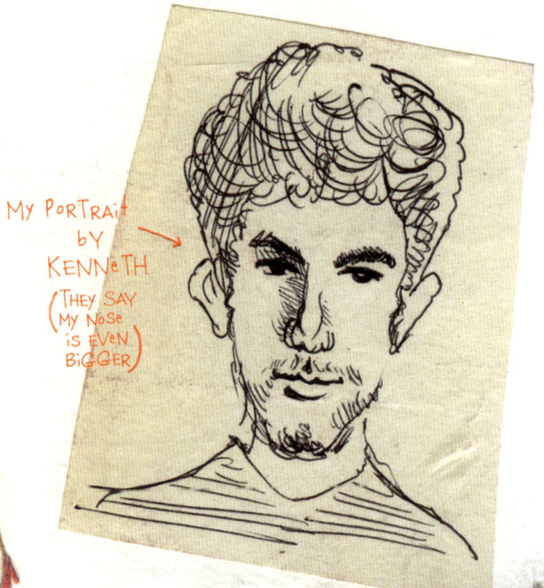

MY PORTRAIT
BY KENNETH
(THEY SAY
MY NOSE
IS EVEN
BIGGER)

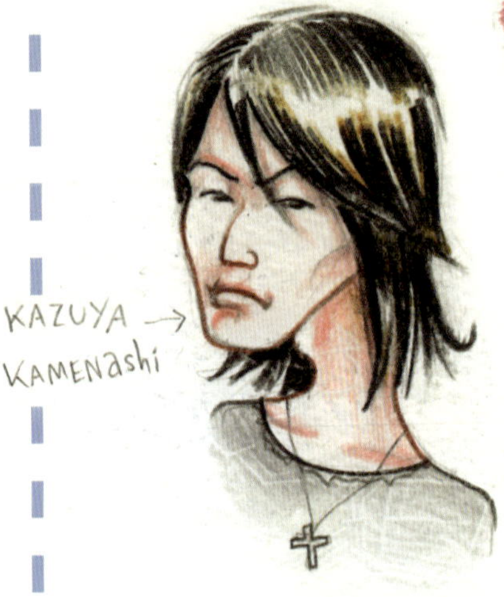

KAZUYA
KAMENASHI

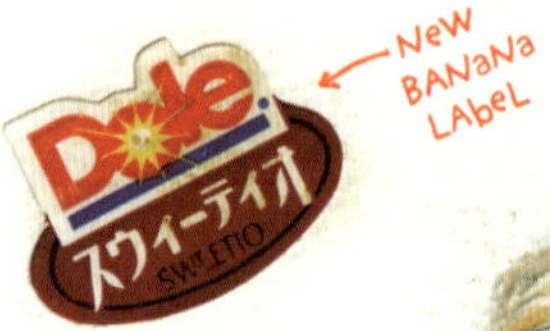

New
BANANA
LABEL

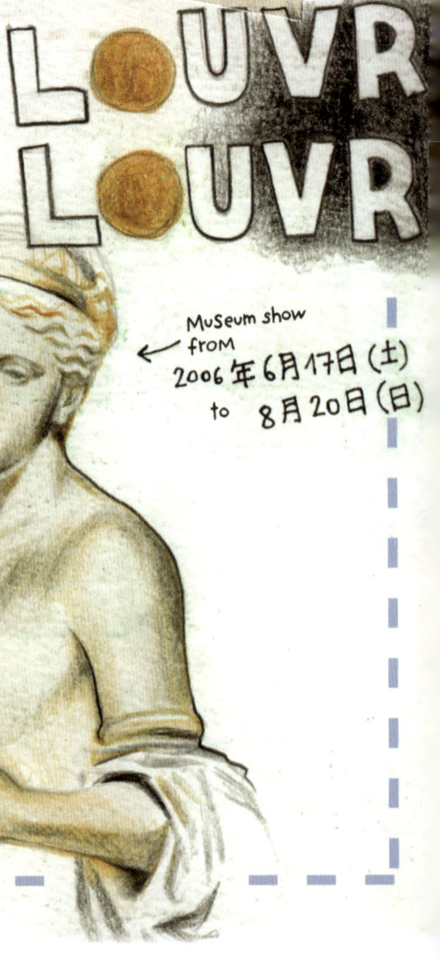

LOUVR
LOUVR

Museum show
from
2006年6月17日(土)
to 8月20日(日)

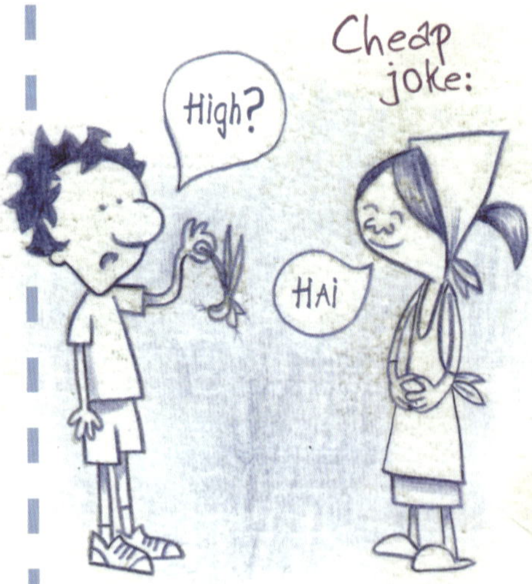

Cheap joke:

High?

HAi

interlude

SMAP 2006

BLACK CIRCLES, DOUBLE CHINS, AND HAIR TRANSFORMED. SPORT and MUSIC ASSEMBLING PEOPLE (?)

KIMURA TAKUYA — Voted some time ago "Japan's Most Handsome Man." Looks a lot like a woman. Sometimes even like a tired transvestite. (Appears in a lot of ads, among others for Gatsby hair gel...)

SHINGO KATORI — "The Funny One" in the group. The tallest too (as I noticed on the internet).

TSUYOSHI KUSANAGI — "The Second Most Handsome." Has a weird head and, like "Most Handsome," does a lot of ads, movies, TV... Right now is playing a dopey guy in a drama. Suits him well.

MASAHIRO NAKAI — SMAP's boss. Strangely not the most charismatic. I had a hard time drawing him. (not very convincing)

To draw the SMAP people is a perilous exercise, since the styles and faces change so quickly. It's like drawing yogurt.

GORO INAGAKI — The shy one you don't notice. He's had problems with the police, they say. BAD BOY!

SHINZO ABE — The newcomer, discreet, stands out due to his remarkable youth and the somewhat complicated lyrics of his songs. 3rd time I've drawn him!

tsukiji

interlude

"udoN!"

"Who don't?"

START OF
A List of
PoLiceMEN
WHo
DeTAiNeD Me →

NA 120
OH 116
OH 246
MA 305
MA 352
MA 061

Hi 108
Hi 100
KA 058
Ji 204
To 193

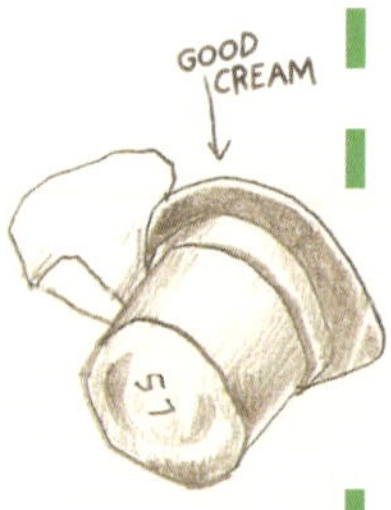

Cheap joke:

free Refills

SHiNJUKU

mister Donut

GOOD CREAM

points south

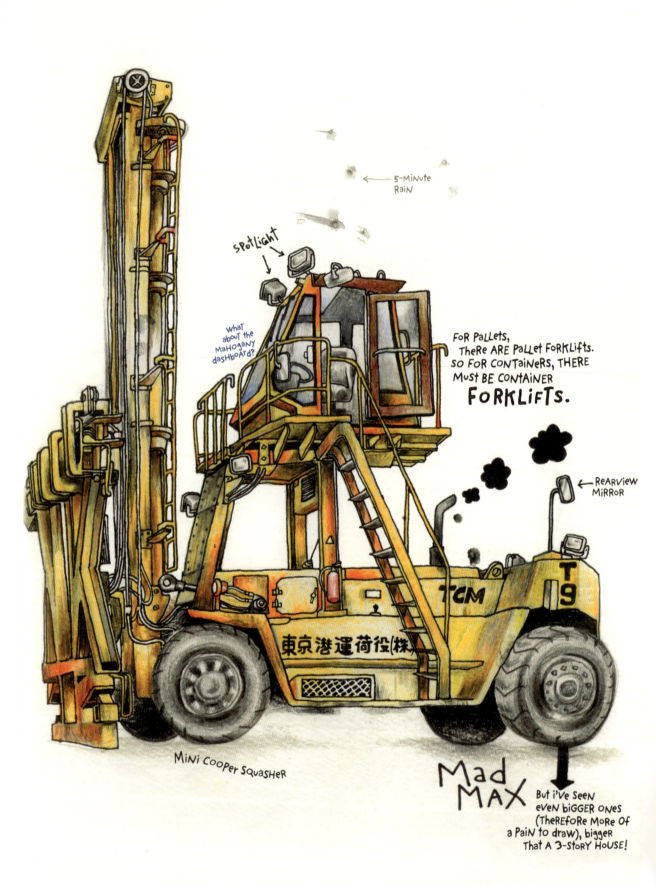

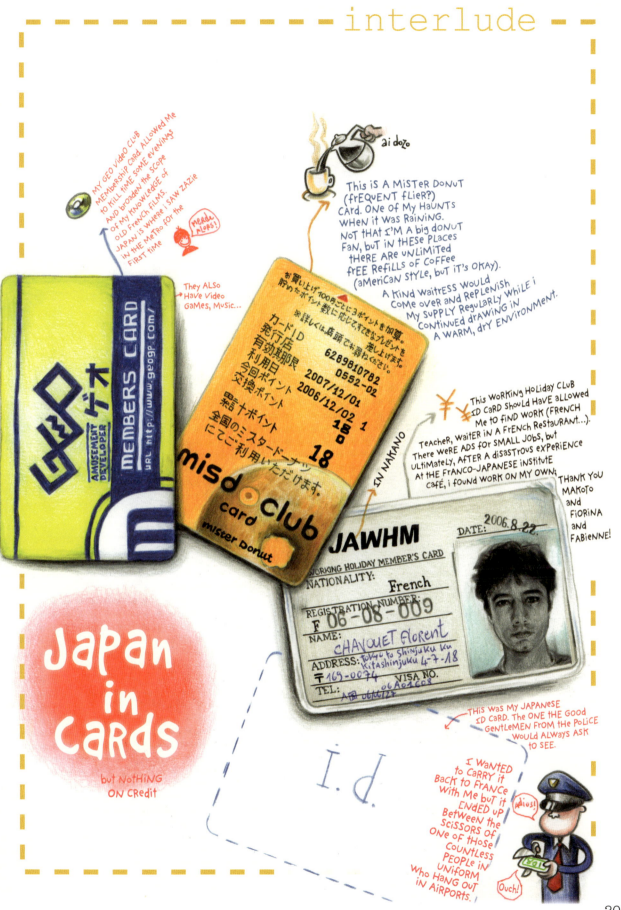

I CONGRATULATE MYSELF ON HAVING SUBSISTED ON LESS THAN ¥900 per day.

I DO NOT CONGRATULATE MYSELF ON KNOWING AS MANY JAPANESE WORDS AS THERE ARE JAPANESE CHEESES.

WELL, YEAH.

IT'S ALREADY OVER?

Bah, I'LL BE BACK...

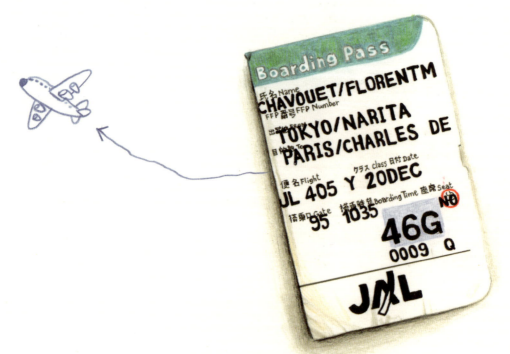

"Books to Span the East and West"

Tuttle Publishing was founded in 1832 in the small New England town of Rutland, Vermont [USA]. Our core values remain as strong today as they were then—to publish best-in-class books which bring people together one page at a time. In 1948, we established a publishing outpost in Japan—and Tuttle is now a leader in publishing English-language books about the arts, languages and cultures of Asia. The world has become a much smaller place today and Asia's economic and cultural influence has grown. Yet the need for meaningful dialogue and information about this diverse region has never been greater. Over the past seven decades, Tuttle has published thousands of books on subjects ranging from martial arts and paper crafts to language learning and literature—and our talented authors, illustrators, designers and photographers have won many prestigious awards. We welcome you to explore the wealth of information available on Asia at **www.tuttlepublishing.com**.